Swamp Explorer

Kathleen Simpson

Contents

Rigby
A Harcourt Achieve Imprint

www.Rigby.com
1-800-531-5015

Introduction

Imagine paddling a canoe through a dark **swamp.** The tangled tree branches above block out most of the sunlight, so you can hardly tell that it's the middle of the day. The thick smell of damp earth and rotting leaves surrounds you as you drift through this wilderness.

Not even a whisper of a breeze stirs the warm, moist air around you, and the stillness is broken only by the distant hoot of an owl. You notice your own reflection on the calm, glassy surface of the river, stained reddish-brown by tree bark and rotting plants. In a world of light and shadows, you drift past colorful flowers that seem to float on the water. PLUNK! A sudden ripple near the water's edge tells you that there is hidden life in this watery place.

3

1 What Is a Swamp?

A swamp is an area of wet, soft land that is covered by water for at least part of the year. The water may be fresh water or salt water, depending on where the swamp is located. Swamps can be found all over the world! Because there is so much water in a swamp, many different plants grow there, providing food for all of the animals that make a swamp their home. A close look at a swamp reveals that it is full of activity.

raccoon

4

One way to think about a swamp is to imagine a giant sponge. When it rains, the soft land takes in the extra water, preventing floods in the surrounding area. Then during the dry season, the extra water that is stored in the swamp flows out to fill rivers and streams. Some plants in the swamp help take away dirt and harmful materials from the water. Many animals find protection among the grasses and trees that grow in a swamp.

How Are Swamps Formed?

Picture yourself at the edge of a swamp, where everything around you is wet—even the air feels damp. Just beyond the swamp, you see a great river. One very rainy spring, many years ago, the river flooded, forming a lake. As time passed, this swamp formed. You wonder what lies beneath the water and what happened to this place. How was this swamp created?

A Swamp Is Formed

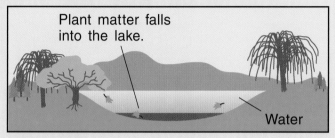

Plant matter falls into the lake.

Water

Leaves, twigs, and other plant parts fall into a flooded area and decay, breaking down slowly and filling up the lake with soil.

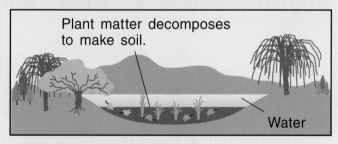

Plant matter decomposes to make soil.

Water

Over time grasses and other plants take root in the soil, and the lake becomes a **marsh.** A marsh is like a swamp, yet it has few trees or shrubs.

Trees take root in shallow water.

Soil fills the lake.

More plants fall into the water and decay, making the water in the marsh even shallower. When the water is shallow enough, trees take root there, and a swamp is formed.

2 Are All Swamps the Same?

All swamps are wetlands with many different kinds of plants and animals, yet they aren't all alike. The features of a swamp often depend upon its climate and location, as well as on the kind of life that is found there.

Cypress Swamps

When most people think of a swamp, they probably imagine a dark, mysterious place filled with muddy water and old, twisted, moss-covered trees. Cypress swamps, which are named for the bald cypress trees that grow there, look something like this. Nearby rivers and streams flood the cypress swamp with fresh water for several months of the year.

Knobby structures called "knees" grow from the underwater roots of cypress trees.

Cypress Trees

Cypress trees have unusual root systems, which grow mostly under fresh water. However, some of the roots stick up out of the water, helping the trees get the air they need. The trunks of some cypress trees are very wide—so wide that several people would have to hold hands to reach all the way around one. Because of its wide base, cypress trees can grow as tall as ten-story buildings, even in soft, wet soil. Cypress trees grow so fast and so tall that they can fill in a swampy area before other trees even begin to grow.

This bullfrog hunts for insects and fish in the shallow water of the swamp.

9

Florida Everglades

The Florida Everglades is a special place, for there is nothing like it anywhere else in the world. Some parts of it are like a swamp, some parts are like a marsh, and most parts of it are like a shallow river. During summer, rainwater collects in Lake Okeechobee and overflows, moving slowly southward. This area of wet, soft land provides a home for countless plants and animals.

Lake Okeechobee, located in Florida, covers more than 700 square miles but is only about 12 feet deep, on average.

The Everglades includes the largest freshwater marsh in the world. This "river of grass," as it is often called, flows over a hundred miles, all the way to Florida Bay. Much of the marshland that makes up the Everglades is covered with sawgrass, a plant whose long slender leaves have sharp edges like the teeth of a saw. Watch out! These teeth keep animals from eating the grass and are sharp enough to cut the clothing and skin of anyone who gets too close. Sawgrass is important to the marsh because its sturdy roots and stems hold the wet soil in place, and it provides a place for birds to nest safely as well.

Mangrove Swamps

Some swamps are not formed by overflowing rivers, but by flooding seas. Most trees can't grow in salty seawater, yet the mangrove tree has special roots and leaves that get rid of salt and allow it to adapt to sea water. Seeds from faraway mangrove trees drift in the ocean for up to a year before they take root in salty mud at the edge of the sea. Mangrove swamps are found in warm tropical regions, such as along the coast of Vietnam.

The roots of the mangrove tree twist and turn over each other, making this swamp a safe, strong home for many creatures. Great clusters of oysters and sponges cling to these roots and become food for thousands of other sea creatures, from tiny shrimp to large fish, such as tarpon.

When the ocean tide is out and the water is low, the tangled roots of the mangrove can be seen above water. In addition to protecting the animals of the swamp, these strong roots also keep the land from washing away during powerful storms.

oysters and sponges

3 Swamp Dwellers

Imagine that you are exploring a swamp. *Buzzz*—a mosquito hums past your ear and around your head before landing on your arm. SLAP! You scare it away, and it zips back to its muddy home. From the trees above you, birds call out noisily, warning each other that you are nearby. You hear something moving in the tall grass, and then—splash! You look up just in time to see an alligator disappear into the dark water. A bullfrog croaks beside your canoe, and a deer crashes through the trees behind you. The swamp is alive with creatures who call it home! Because there is plenty of food in the swamp, animals of all kinds find what they need to survive here.

When the giant water bug hunts for food in the water, it takes an air bubble with it, so that it can breathe. It eats tadpoles, small frogs, and fish.

deer

Furry Animals in Swamps

You hear a noise in the bushes, and a ring-tailed raccoon comes into view. He stops at the edge of the river, hoping to catch a fish for lunch. Two playful otters splash about in the water, and a muskrat swims by, ready to duck beneath the surface at the first sign of danger.

Larger animals wander toward the swamp in search of food, and then retreat to higher ground to rest. Fierce, fast-moving bobcats prowl the edges of swamps in search of small animals to eat. Black bears are among the largest animals found in swamps. They eat a variety of plants and animals, including berries, grass, insects, frogs, and fish. If you try, you might see one of these animals hunting for a meal.

black bear

Birds in Swamps

You may notice a flash of colorful feathers or a noisy chirping that tells you there are birds nearby. Many small birds live in trees and bushes in the swamp, feeding on berries and insects.

Several kinds of bigger birds have also **adapted** well to the watery surroundings of the swamp. Some of these birds have long legs for standing in the shallow water. The white ibis waits quietly for a fish to swim by and then uses its thin, sharp beak to grab it.

Long legs and a sharp beak help the white ibis adapt to living in a swamp.

Some birds that are passing through on their journey from one place to another also stop to feed in the swamp. Many kinds of birds use swamps as a nesting place where they lay their eggs and raise their young.

Reptiles in Swamps

You hear a sound in the grass, and a snake creeps out from under a bush. Many snakes that live in the swamp are harmless, but a few are dangerous. The poisonous cottonmouth, for example, captures its food by sneaking up on another animal.

Alligators are the strongest, most frightening animals in the swamp, and they have lived there for the last 200 million years. These reptiles have short legs for walking on land and strong tails for swimming, so they have adapted well to life in the swamp. Alligators hunt for food at night and will eat almost anything, including raccoons, fish, frogs, turtles, insects, birds, and other alligators.

cottonmouth

Amazing Alligators

- An alligator can spend several hours underwater without ever coming up for air.
- Alligators may look a bit clumsy on land, but they can actually run as fast as 30 miles per hour. So watch out, for they can run faster than you!
- An alligator has about 80 teeth, and when one falls out, a new one grows in its place.

4 Food Chain

A snail eats a leaf while a woodpecker tap-tap-taps on a tree trunk, looking for tasty insects. A snake steals an egg from a blue heron's nest while the mother bird is out catching fish. The process in which one living thing eats another is called a **food chain.**

Living things in swamps depend on each other. Green plants, which are also called **producers,** use sunlight and a gas called carbon dioxide to produce their own food. Tiny creatures that feed on dead plants and animals provide food for shrimp, bugs, crabs, and other small animals. These, in turn, are dinner for frogs, snakes, alligators, deer, and hundreds of other **predators** that hunt and eat other animals. In this way, the energy produced by plants is passed along the chain from one creature to another.

Did You Know?

Some plants eat animals! The pitcher plant gets some of its food from insects that it catches with special, pitcher-shaped leaves. Pitcher plants are found in many freshwater swamps.

Food chains are different from one swamp to the next because the plants and animals that live in each swamp are different. Picture a mangrove swamp. How do all of the creatures who live there survive?

Eating to Survive

Bacteria and **fungi** grow on dead plants and animals in the swamp, breaking them down into material that helps the mangrove grow. As the mangrove grows, some of its leaves drop off and decay.

Crabs and shrimp feed on bits of decaying leaves.

An alligator catches an animal such as a bird, a raccoon, or a turtle for supper.

The shrimp are
eaten by fish.

These fish swim among the
roots of the mangrove trees.

Animals like snakes and raccoons
steal the eggs of some birds in
the swamp.

Herons and other birds
eat these fish.

What Happens if the Food Chain Is Broken?

Imagine that you are a farmer who lives on the edge of a small swamp. You know that the many birds in the swamp help keep insects from eating your crops, and you enjoy watching them hunt for fish. One day, an alligator eats one of the birds, and you think, "I should get rid of that alligator." Is this really a good idea?

storks and pelicans

Remember, alligators also eat other animals, such as raccoons and turtles. If the alligators were not present, there would be more raccoons and turtles in the swamp, and these animals would eat more fish. They would take food from the birds that you enjoy so much, and some of the birds might go hungry and die. If there were fewer birds in the swamp, they would not be able to protect your crops by eating dangerous insects.

Every plant and animal in the food chain affects every other plant and animal, including you!

People are part of the swamp food chain, too. These men from Brazil are selling the fish they caught in a swamp.

5 Exploring a Swamp

The swamp is a wonderful place to learn about wildlife, but it is also a special system and a home to many creatures. These wild animals like to be left alone, so a swamp must always be explored very carefully. In addition, many plants in a swamp can be dangerous to humans, so explorers must protect the swamp—and themselves!

Swamp Explorer's Safety Checklist

✔ Wear sturdy shoes—never sandals—to protect your feet from biting snakes and insects.

✔ Wear sunscreen, a hat, long sleeves, long pants, and socks to protect you from mosquitoes and sunburn.

✔ Be prepared for surprises—always carry a watch, a compass, a map, a flashlight, and a water bottle.

✔ Avoid getting too close to wild animals, and never touch one.

✔ Don't touch plants in the swamp unless an expert guide tells you that it's safe.

✔ Always have an adult with you when you explore a swamp, and stay on trails that are clearly marked.

✔ Never leave food or trash behind in the swamp, and don't take anything from the swamp when you leave.

6 How Can We Take Care of Swamps?

Are you wondering what you can do to protect our swamps? You are already doing something important—you are learning about the balance of life in these wetlands. If you are lucky enough to visit a swamp, you must look and listen carefully without harming what lives there.

Scientists who study swamps help us understand how important these special areas are. One way that some people help care for swamps is by creating laws to protect them. Many groups have worked to stop people from hunting animals that are in danger of dying out and from destroying the places where they live. In many areas, there are laws against draining swamps or filling in wetlands.

Alligator Nurseries

Experts all over the world are working to save the Chinese alligator that is, sadly, running out of space to live, just like the American crocodile. There are now fewer than 150 Chinese alligators left in the wild. The good news is that Chinese alligators do well in zoos and other "alligator nurseries."

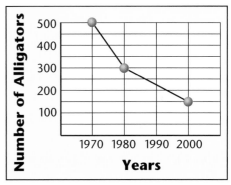

Estimated Numbers of Wild Chinese Alligators

Number of Alligators

500 400 300 200 100

1970 1980 1990 2000

Years

29

Rebuilding Lost Swamps

Scientists are finding that sometimes it is possible to bring swamps that have disappeared back to life. A project to replant mangroves along the coast of Vietnam has been very successful. People who live in the area were given tiny mangrove seedlings, along with instructions on how to plant and care for them. Not only are the mangrove swamps coming back to life, but people are also learning how important it is to maintain these areas. Another project is underway in Florida to bring back the Everglades by creating thousands of acres of new marshes.

In the United States, in Vietnam, and throughout the world, people are trying to save their swamps and protect the plants and animals that live there. Swamps are special places where amazing creatures live, and that's why we need to protect them.

People in Vietnam plant mangrove seedlings, hoping to bring the mangrove swamps back to life.

Glossary

adapt to adjust to one's surroundings

bacteria very tiny living things found in air, water, and soil

food chain a link created when one living thing is eaten by another living thing, which is eaten by an even larger living thing

fungi a plant that doesn't have leaves and grows in dark, warm, wet places

marsh an area of soft, wet land

predator a living thing that catches and eats other animals

producer a living thing that makes food from minerals, water, and sunlight

swamp an area of land that is very wet and sometimes covered in water

Index